D0257221

Role Play

Ready, Steady, Play!

Series Editor: Sandy Green

Guaranteed fun for children and practitioners alike, the Ready, Steady, Play! series provides lively and stimulating activities for children.

Each book focuses on one specific aspect of play offering clear and detailed guidance on how to plan and enjoy wonderful play experiences with minimum fuss and maximum success.

Each book in the Ready, Steady, Play! series includes advice on:

- How to prepare the children and the play space
- What equipment and materials are needed
- How much time is needed to prepare and carry out the activity
- How many staff are required
- How to communicate with parents and colleagues

Ready, Steady, Play! helps you to:

- Develop activities easily, using suggested guidelines
- Ensure that health and safety issues are taken into account
- Plan play that links to the early years curriculum
- Broaden your understanding of early years issues

Early years practitioners and students on early years courses and parents looking for simple, excellent ideas for creative play will love these books!

Other titles in the series

Books, Stories and Puppets 1-84312-148-4 Green
Construction 1-84312-098-4 Boyd
Creativity 1-84312-076-3 Green
Displays and Interest Tables 1-84312-267-7 Olpin
Festivals 1-84312-101-8 Hewitson
Food and Cooking 1-84312-100-X Green
Music and Singing 1-84312-276-6 Durno
Nature, Living and Growing 1-84312-114-X Harper
Play Using Natural Materials 1-84312-099-2 Howe

OLDHAM COLLEGE

BARCODE...... CT01361
CL: No. 372.21 GRE
DA APRIL 2010

Role Play

Sandy Green

David Fulton Publishers

David Fulton Publishers Ltd
The Chiswick Centre, 414 Chiswick High Road, London W4 5TF

www.fultonpublishers.co.uk

First published in Great Britain in 2005 by David Fulton Publishers

10 9 8 7 6 5 4 3 2 1

Note: The right of Sandy Green to be identified as the author of this work has been
asserted by her in accordance with the Copyright, Designs and Patents Act 1988.

David Fulton Publishers is a division of Granada Learning Limited, part of ITV plc.

Copyright © Sandy Green 2005

British Library Cataloguing in Publication Data
A catalogue record for this book is available from the British Library.

ISBN 1-84312-147-6

The materials in this publication may be photocopied only for use within the
purchasing organisation. Otherwise, all rights reserved. No part of this publication
may be reproduced, stored in a retrieval system or transmitted, in any form or by any
means, electronic, mechanical, photocopying, or otherwise, without the prior
permission of the publishers.

Typeset by FiSH Books, London
Printed and bound in Great Britain

Contents

Role Play

Welcome to *Role Play*, an exciting new publication which is part of the Ready, Steady, Play! series.

Get ready to enjoy a range of activities with your children, which will stimulate their all-round development.

The Ready, Steady, Play! books will help boost the confidence of new practitioners by providing information and fun ideas to support planning and preparation. The series will also consolidate and extend learning for the more experienced practitioner. Attention is drawn to health and safety, and the role of the adult is addressed.

How to use this book

Role Play is divided into four main sections.

Section 1 provides background information on imaginative play, and discusses both structured and free expression play. Ideas are provided for planning and preparing a stimulating environment, together with health and safety issues, the importance of cultural diversity, and the role of the adult during the play. It ends with a brief summary of some early years theorists' views on the value of imaginative/role play.

Section 2 presents a range of visual images to help stimulate discussion with children. Each photograph is linked to a place or a situation familiar to most. These images may be used to help jog memories of familiar experiences and as prompts to help form the basis on which children can build ideas for their role play. Practitioners can best support children through careful questioning, encouraging them to reflect and suggest, therefore involving them in the planning of their play.

The third section offers practical suggestions for setting up themed role-play areas. There are also ideas for making a range of props, both with and for the children. Some commercially available examples have also been included.

The section of photocopiable pages at the end of the book provides a selection of useful ideas to support role play. For example, templates for making masks, instructions for tying a sari and a turban, together with recipe and menu cards for café or restaurant play, and basic patterns for dressing-up clothes.

So read on, and enjoy ... Ready, Steady, Play!

Sandy Green
Series editor

Acknowledgements

Thanks are due to the following companies for the use of their products and photographs throughout this book:

- East–West Education
- Stompers
- Shops and businesses of Moorland Road shopping centre, Bath
- Noah's Ark Nursery School, Midsomer Norton
- Broomhill Infants School, Brislington, Bristol

Series acknowledgement

The series editor would like to thank the children, parents and staff at:

- The Nursery and Reception class, Wadebridge County Primary School, Wadebridge, Cornwall
- Happy Days Day Nursery, Wadebridge, Cornwall
- Snapdragons Nursery, Weston, Bath, Somerset
- Snapdragons Nursery, Grosvenor, Bath, Somerset
- Tadpoles Nursery, Combe Down, Bath, Somerset

for allowing us to take photographs of their excellent provision, resources and displays.

Also to John and Jake Green, Jasmine and Eva for their help throughout the series, and to Nina, Margaret and Ben at David Fulton Publishers for their patience, enthusiasm and support.

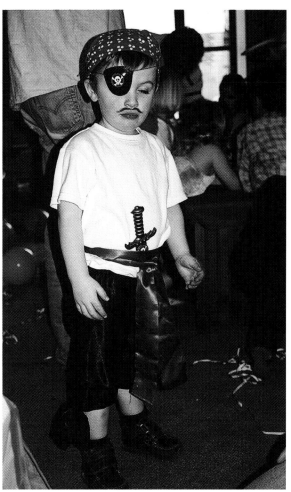

Introduction

What is role play? Why is it important?

Children start to role play from the moment they begin to imitate what they see around them. This imitative play helps them to make sense of their environment and to move on in their understanding of how things happen, and what it feels like to do something different or to be somebody else. They gain confidence through the opportunity to organise their own play, taking decisions and considering the outcomes of what they are doing. Their social skills are enhanced as they practise dressing themselves and as they play with others, negotiating ideas and sharing resources.

Ideally, all early years settings would offer opportunities for role play at every session. This might vary from the freedom to dress up and be somebody or something else, through to a more structured environment where a theme has been suggested by either the adult or (more importantly) by the child, for example, post office play (see pages 46–47).

Whenever possible, provide 'free' role-play opportunities alongside any themed area, and enjoy observing the children as they develop their imagination, moving between 'free' play and 'themed' play, often broadening the scope of their play considerably.

Technically, role play can also include the enjoyment of small world toys, where the children direct the action rather than taking on a role themselves. This book, however, focuses on role play in which children are actively participating.

The most usually found 'free' role-play area is the 'home' corner. While this play experience gives important opportunities for children to explore their own lives and those of their family and other primary carers and important people, these experiences may be built on further and extended to incorporate many of the situations and environments children enjoy regularly (e.g. shop play), and on special occasions (e.g. café play or travel experiences), outside of the home environment.

Ideally, early years practitioners will involve their children in the development of any specifically themed role-play setting, planning the area with them, incorporating their suggestions whenever practicable, and involving them in gathering and preparing resources. This can be an ideal way to get parents involved too, through the provision of objects and artefacts from home.

Find ways of explaining the value of role play to parents through your notice-boards, newsletters and so on, emphasising the opportunities the children have for developing language, mathematical skills and understanding in general through these learning experiences.

Try displaying examples of how role play helps children to reach aspects of each of the six main learning areas. This will help parents to appreciate its value more fully.

Role play does not have to mean complicated structures with commercial resources. Simple items such as large cardboard boxes (e.g. from washing machines) make wonderful props. Children have amazing imaginations if they are allowed to use them. They do not need replicas of everything we as adults use in our commercially led lives. They are usually very happy to simply pretend. The richest learning role-play environments are those which are child-centred, supported by informed and interested adults (see pages 50–74 for ideas for simply produced role-play props).

The role of the adult

The role of the adult is to support and extend understanding through sensitive interaction, and also to maintain a safe and uncluttered environment, supporting the children in their management of this environment. As an adult you should not be organising or directing the play but simply providing the opportunity, modelling role behaviours and use of resources as you feel appropriate.

Adult involvement in role-play settings will often be as a customer (e.g. shops and cafés), a passenger (e.g. buses and planes), a client (e.g. hairdressers and estate agents), or a patient (e.g. hospitals, doctors' surgeries, clinics and veterinary surgeries). It is important that you accept your 'role' and join in with the children's ideas and scenarios, rather than imposing adult-led thinking and expectation on the play. You can, however, enhance the learning for the children by introducing and re-enforcing language appropriate to the current setting, and by open questioning. This will help to encourage creative and descriptive vocabulary.

Planning and preparation of the environment

When planning the environment, it is important to consider:

- The space available for role play.
- The likely impact of the play on other activities within the setting.
- The children's own ideas.
- The resources needed to stimulate and support children in their play.
- The numbers of children able to role play safely at any one time.
- The children's level of understanding of any themed role-play activity.

Whenever possible, discuss with the children what should be included in a role-play area if it is to be linked to a specific theme. The photographs on pages 13–22 are designed to help initiate discussion of places familiar to many children, leading to an exploration of ideas and the eventual play area being resourced with the children's thinking and involvement. It can be invaluable to get into the habit of collecting 'useful' items such as business cards, take-away menus, posters for walls and so on for use during appropriate role play.

D0101351

During discussion support children as they reflect on past experiences, for example, what happened when they went to the post office (weighing a parcel, sticking a stamp on), or how they located their new book at the bookshop (books in different sections, authors' names being alphabetically set out). Children will be able to re-enact these scenarios with your help.

Support them also in thinking about what they may find in and around a specified environment. For example, why might people go to a veterinary surgery? What would they take with them? What can you buy there? What does a vet do?

You will need to consider:

- Where you might acquire items.
- How you could provide an alternative or made item.
- Which children need to see the use of certain resources modelled for them.

Equality of opportunity issues

As you gather the resources for a role-play area, it is important for you to ensure that cultural diversity is taken into account. This is of equal importance whether you live in an area of limited or rich diversity. The parents of each culture represented within your setting will be a wonderful and ideal source of ideas of what you might include, and will usually be pleased to supply and/or suggest items that are normally found in their homes or used within their culture. This involvement also acknowledges that you value their input into their child's learning and demonstrates your interest in their culture.

Health and safety

As with any aspect of play, the resources you provide need to be safe, robust and appropriate. Children will gain greater satisfaction in their play through resources that enable them to explore the environment fully in an unhindered manner. Whenever possible, provide equipment that is as real as is practical. Many items can be made (see pages 50–74 for examples).

When acquiring props from parents and carers, ensure they are fully checked for any defects. They are only a boost to your stock of resources and artefacts if suitability and safety are guaranteed.

Consideration is needed regarding the storage and presentation of resources. Think about the following:

■ Where will they be stored?
■ How safe is the storage?
■ Will all children be able to access the resources safely and easily?
■ How will resources be stored long term?

It can be useful to store items according to specific themes (e.g. garden centres, travel agents). You can then add items to a theme easily whenever you acquire them.

Spatial awareness

Think about the space you are providing for the children to play 'in role'. Is it sufficient for several children to play together? What limitation might you need to implement? Children are very good at working within boundaries if these boundaries are explained to them and upheld. Explain to them why you have had to limit numbers to play in the area at any one time. Ensure that there is a fair system for taking turns if role-play opportunities are particularly sought after.

Many children love to wear dressing-up clothes while playing in other areas. Whenever practical, encourage opportunities for this type of free expression and enjoyment.

Themed play

Setting up themed role-play areas enables practitioners to fully integrate children's imaginative play into the current topic or general theme if they feel it will be beneficial to their learning. Children's understanding may be built upon further by reading books linked to the theme, to include both stories and information texts.

When relevant, invite a visitor from the local community to talk about his or her role (e.g. a postman, veterinary nurse, lollipop person, hairdresser or health visitor).

Try setting up supportive activities that focus on a specific aspect of the role play (e.g. plaiting activities (hairdresser play), making parcels (post office play), making bird feeders (garden centre or pet-shop play).

Ask yourself:

- Whose parents can offer a relevant skill or a breadth of extra knowledge?
- Is a linked visit possible?
- How can you best record images of the play for reflection at a later stage?

Whenever possible, allow the children to take the lead and develop resources to support the diversity and creativity in their play.

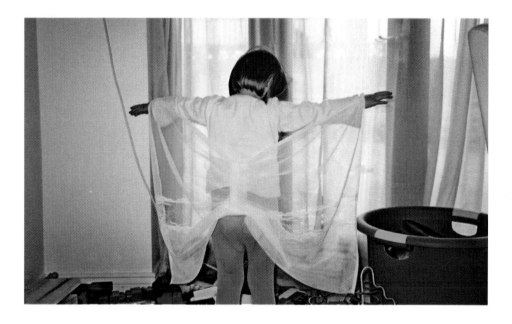

Storytelling as a mini-drama

Role play can be enjoyed as a whole group activity with an adult guiding the children through a story, rhyme or scenario, supporting them as they take part in joint actions and responses.

This type of experience can help consolidate the sequence of stories for some children (i.e. the 'introduction, the main body of the story or process, followed by the conclusion – the happy ending'). It can also help less confident children feel able to take part in a group activity that is both fun and 'non-threatening'. Often, no resources are needed, but at times simple props may be considered useful.

Simple stories to dramatise as a group could include traditional tales such as 'The Three Billy Goats Gruff' or 'The Three Little Pigs', as each has a wide range of suitable aspects to perform (e.g. 'trip-trapping' over imaginary bridges and 'huffing and puffing' houses down. Popular stories such as *We're Going on a Bear Hunt* by Michael Rosen are always great fun too.

A useful range of books that offers detailed guidance on group drama activities has been written by Jo Boulton and Judith Ackroyd. Details of these books can be found on page 75.

Links with theory

Imaginative role play enables children to act out real and imagined experiences, both familiar and unknown. A number of theorists have supported this type of play, placing value on its contribution to a child's learning and general development.

Jean Piaget

Jean Piaget considered play as the means by which children come to terms with the world. He believed that play was a way in which children were able to combine experience, knowledge and understanding. Between the ages of two and seven children are in what Piaget called the pre-operational period (i.e. they play symbolically). This is regularly seen during role play, for example, a large box may become a car, or the area underneath a table becomes a house. Children use their prior knowledge and experience to inform all aspects of their play, and in role-play situations, as their knowledge and understanding develops, so does the complexity of their play.

Lev Vygotsky

Lev Vygotsky placed emphasis on the importance of social interactions, a central aspect of role-play experiences. He saw the role of the adult as important in helping children to develop, and sensitive intervention or modelling of actions during imaginative play are very relevant here.

Sigmund Freud

Sigmund Freud considered that play was a means of children acting out their fears, enabling them to cope with these fears. Many children have been observed acting out situations that may be causing them anxiety, for example, family discord, or the arrival of a new baby in the house. Freud, and later Erik Erikson, considered that if children could act out their fears within a 'safe' environment, they would have a greater chance of coping with their fears, disappointment and anger, and perhaps even a sense of failure, in the future.

Susan Isaacs

Like Freud, Susan Isaacs valued imaginative play for its role in a child's emotional development, allowing children to move into their imagination to avoid difficult real-life events, and also to 'escape' back from their imagination into reality, regaining the security of familiar situations.

Tina Bruce

More recently, Tina Bruce (1991) drew up her well-respected list of twelve features of free-flow play, which sum up the best of play (including role-play) experiences. In Feature 8 she refers to children drawing on their experience 'from the basis of both shared and personal knowledge'.

She goes on to say that 'through their firsthand experiences, they [children] have imagined, explored, practised and become competent and proficient'.

From these brief snapshots of theory we can see that the value of role play has been identified and applauded by theorists both past and contemporary.

Discussion resources

The following section provides a range of photographs linked to places familiar to most children, together with some that they may not have seen before. These may be used to stimulate discussion with children, broadening their knowledge of both their local and extended environment, and providing a starting point for planning themed role play.

Where might this be?

Where is the baby? What is happening?

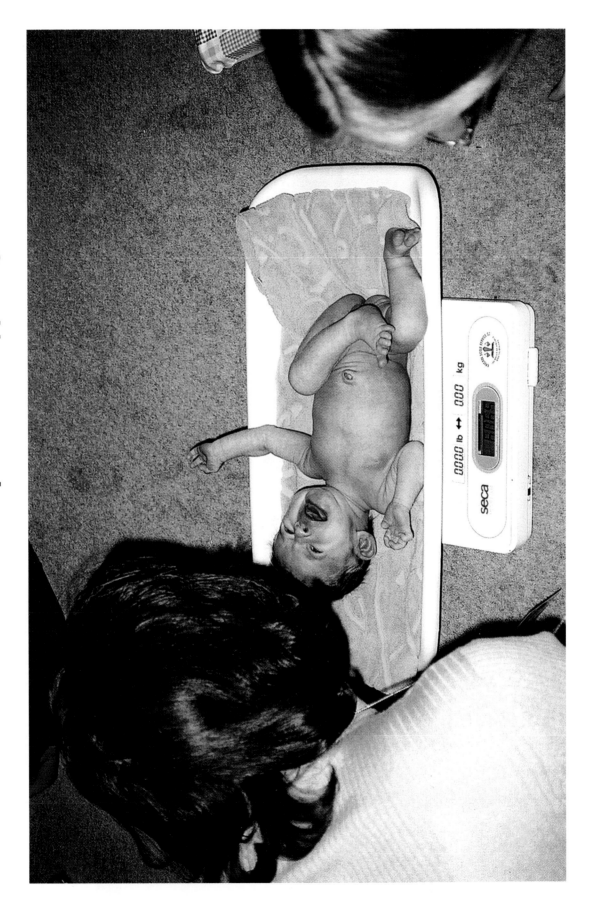

What happens at the veterinary centre?

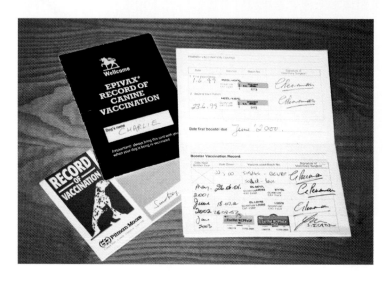

What sort of shop is this?

What shop are these linked to?

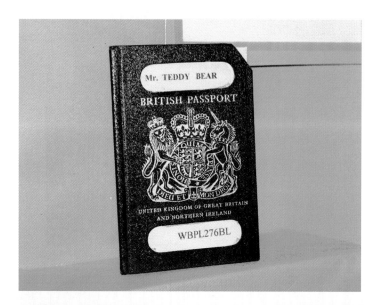

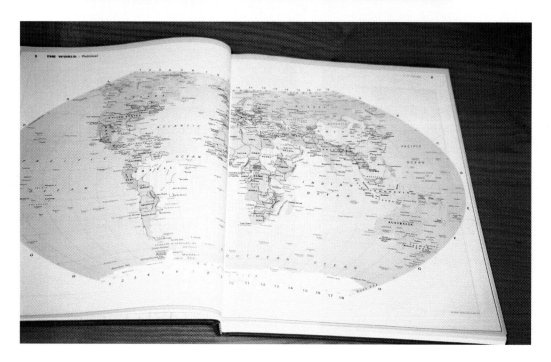

Have you ever been into a bookshop?

What shop is this? What else could you buy there?

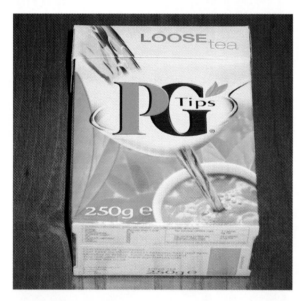

When might you buy flowers?

Have you ever been to a garden centre?

Activities/role-play themes

The following pages contain twelve different suggestions for planning and setting up a themed role-play area. Each activity follows a standard format to ensure ease of planning and implementation:

- suggested resources
- the aim(s)/concept(s)
- process/activities
- vocabulary/discussion
- extension ideas
- links to the Foundation Stage Curriculum.

Key to Foundation Stage Curriculum abbreviations:

(SS) Stepping stones

ELG Early learning goals

PSE Personal, social and emotional development

CLL Communication, language and literacy

MD Mathematical development

KUW Knowledge and understanding of the world

PD Physical development

CD Creative development

A summary of aims generic to all role play

In setting up role play you provide children with a wonderful range of opportunities. Each opportunity could be set out as an individual and valid aim for the play.

To list them all each time in the following pages of suggested role-play themes would become cumbersome; therefore they have been summarised below. Refer back to these points as you develop role play with your children to help you identify opportunities for assessment of their progress.

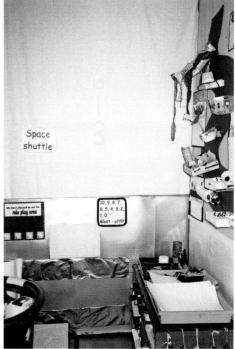

Role play provides children with opportunities:

■ To explore their immediate environment.
■ To act out familiar situations in sequence (e.g. cooking dinner, making tea, going shopping).
■ To find out about the wider environment, including culture, customs and places.
■ To express their concerns, feelings and fears within a secure environment.

- To initiate play, and to share play experiences with others.
- To lead, and to follow.
- To use their developing language skills to socialise and interact.
- To write for a purpose (e.g. labels, signposts, food orders, letters for posting).
- To handle money in practical situations (e.g. buying and selling items, giving and receiving change).

- To classify, make calculations and solve problems (e.g. Have we got enough cups? How many more chairs are needed?).

Dressing up enables children to:

- Develop manipulative dexterity as they put on clothing items, both familiar and new, and to learn to fasten zips, buttons, sashes, toggles and so on.
- Take on the role of others, at times helping them to clarify their understanding of prior experiences.
- Use their imagination.
- Represent familiar situations through imitation and mimicry.

ACTIVITY 1 A café

Resources you will need

- Child-size tables and chairs
- Cups, saucers, plates and dishes
- Notebooks and pens
- Vases of flowers – real or artificial
- Till, money, purses
- Food – pretend or made with salt dough (see page 62)
- Washing-up bowl
- Tea towels
- Cooking pans, a wok, a griddle
- Cooking utensils
- Serviettes
- Pictures for the walls
- Curtains for the windows

- Table cloths
- Cutlery
- Menus
- Pot plants

Aim/concept

For children to learn about social meal sharing, and the use of social conventions in giving and taking food orders and making and taking payment

Process

- Look at pictures of a café with the children.
- Discuss who has been to a café. When? Why? What did they eat?
- Discuss menus – choosing and writing down the order.
- Ask the children what they will need to set up a café within the setting.
- Write a menu with the children. You may need to scribe it for them (see example on page 70). Photocopy your menu several times, and if possible get copies laminated.
- In small groups help the children set up the café area, using the resources available.
- Ensure that all children have opportunities to play in the café.
- Encourage them to play different roles. Model actions and gestures for them.
- Help them to use money to pay and give change.
- Encourage the children to decide where their café might be (e.g. in the high street, by the sea).

Vocabulary/discussion

- Talk about different types of cafés and eating places. Discuss textures, flavours and types of food

Group size

4–6

Extension ideas

Have a themed café, e.g.

1. An Indian restaurant.
2. An Italian pasta house.
3. A Chinese restaurant.
4. Make it a 'take-away'.
5. Add balloons, streamers and so on to give it a party atmosphere.
6. Try making false windows on the wall with an outside 'view' (e.g of the sea if it is a seaside café). See activity on page 60.
7. Let the children take turns to have their snacks or lunch in the café.
8. Read books about eating out (e.g. *The Tiger Who Came to Tea* by Judith Kerr).

Links to Foundation Stage Curriculum

PSE	Display high levels of involvement in activities (SS)
ELG	Be confident to try new activities, initiate ideas and speak in a familiar group
CLL	Initiate conversation, attend to and take account of what others say, and use talk to resolve disagreements (SS)
ELG	Interact with others, negotiating plans and activities and taking turns in conversations
CLL	Use talk, actions and objects to recall and relive past experiences (SS)
ELG	Use talk to imagine and re-create roles and experiences
MD	Use some number names and number language spontaneously (SS)
ELG	Use developing mathematical ideas and methods to solve practical problems
CD	Pretend that one object represents another, especially when objects have characteristics in common (SS)
ELG	Use imagination in art and design, music, dance, imaginative and role play and stories
CD	Express and communicate ideas, thoughts and feelings by using imaginative and role play (ELG)

2 A hospital

Resources you will need

- Child-size beds, chairs and tables
- A screen if possible
- Nurses' and doctors' outfits for both boys and girls
- Nurses' capes and caps
- Hospital-style gowns
- Doll-size cots and beds
- Dolls and teddies
- Medical kits – as realistic as possible
- Child-size blood-pressure cuff
- Unwanted (sterile) syringes (no needles obviously)
- Trays for laying out equipment for 'operations'
- Bandages
- Hospital name bands
- Vase of flowers
- Clipboards with paper and pens for writing temperature charts and so on

Aim/concept

To support emotional security as children play out expectations and experiences of hospital stays and appointments, enabling them to handle and investigate equipment and resources

Process

- Look at pictures of a hospital with the children.
- Who has been to hospital? When was this? Did they stay in? Did they visit somebody? What was it like? How did they get there? Has anyone had an X-ray?
- Discuss what and who the children might see in a hospital. How do they know if someone is a nurse or a doctor?
- Why do people need to go to hospital?
- What do the nurses and doctors do?
- Encourage the children to suggest what they would need to set up a hospital corner.
- Help them to set it up.
- Support their play through careful questioning, introducing new ideas to them as appropriate – Are you the visitor today, Joseph? Does the nurse need to take your temperature today, Marlene? Where will the new baby sleep? Is Justin asleep or has he had an anaesthetic?
- Be ready to answer questions honestly, but at a level appropriate to the child's age.

Vocabulary/discussion

- Provide correct names for medical equipment and procedures: stethoscope, tweezers, thermometer, operation, X-ray
- Talk about reasons for going to hospital: outpatient appointments, feeling poorly, broken legs
- Talk about body parts and functions
- Talk about the importance of cleanliness and sterile items
- Talk about tablets and medicines, and the dangers of taking them when not prescribed by a doctor

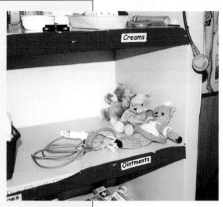

Group size

4–6

Extension ideas

1. Set up a waiting area for 'check-ups'.
2. Make plaster cast models of children's hands, using air-dry clay or papier mâché.
3. Enjoy syringe painting with the children.
4. Read books about going into hospital.
5. Make a large temperature chart to go on the wall, taking teddy's temperature regularly.
6. Use large transparent storage boxes as incubators for 'babies'.
7. Provide a printing activity, using the ends of stethoscopes as printers.
8. Make an X-ray and frame it, and talk about what an X-ray can show.
9. Make a temperature chart and 'take' temperatures.

Links to Foundation Stage Curriculum

PSE	Display high levels of involvement in activities (SS)
ELG	Be confident to try new activities, initiate ideas and speak in a familiar group
CLL	Initiate conversation, attend to and take account of what others say, and use talk to resolve disagreements (SS)
ELG	Interact with others, negotiating plans and activities and taking turns in conversation
CLL	Use talk, actions and objects to recall and relive past experiences (SS)
ELG	Use language to imagine and re-create roles and experiences
KUW	Describe simple features of objects and events (SS)
ELG	Find out about, and identify, some features of living things, objects and events they observe
KUW	Know how to operate simple equipment (SS)
ELG	Find out about and identify the uses of everyday technology
PD	Show awareness of a range of healthy practices with regard to eating, sleeping and hygiene (SS)
ELG	Recognise the importance of keeping healthy and those things which contribute to good health
CD	Pretend that one object represents another, especially when objects have characteristics in common (SS)
ELG	Use imagination in art and design, music, dance, imaginative and role play and stories
CD	Express and communicate ideas, thoughts and feelings by using imaginative and role play (ELG)

ACTIVITY 3 A hairdressers' salon

Resources you will need

- Child-size chairs
- Washing-up bowls to act as basins
- A bucket on a broom handle, embedded in a deep bucket of sand to use as a hairdryer
- Mirrors – always use those with safety surfaces
- Hairdressers' gowns (or capes worn back to front)
- Towels
- Pretend handheld hairdryers and curling tongs or old ones with all electrical parts removed
- Hairbrushes and combs – ensure these are soaked regularly in a disinfectant and rinsed well to help prevent cross-infestation of head lice
- Pretend (completely blunt) plastic scissors
- A variety of hair rollers, decorative combs, scrunchies
- A selection of magazines for clients to look at while they wait
- Cups and saucers
- Posters for the walls showing glamorous people
- A till and money for paying and giving change

Aim/concept

For children to explore ways to take care of themselves, to encourage pride in their appearance, and to have fun

Process

- Look at pictures of hairdressers.
- Who has been to the hairdressers? Whose family members go to one?
- How often do they go? Why is this?
- Talk about hairstyles, discussing the various styles, lengths, cuts and colours of the children's hair.
- Tell them about how you care for your hair.
- How do they care for their hair? Who helps them?
- Support them in thinking about the equipment needed to make a hair salon area.
- Help them to prepare the area and make suitable props.

- Encourage them to take different roles – the client and the hairdresser. Model actions for them as necessary: gowns on 'back to front', towels around shoulders, holding mirrors to show the back view of the hairstyle, offering cups of coffee.
- Help them to use money to pay and give change.

Vocabulary/discussion

- Talk about hairstyles, hair types: straight, curly, thick, fine, blond, black, auburn and so on

Group size

4

Extension ideas

1. Read books about personal hygiene and grooming.
2. Make a chart of different hairstyles and/or hair colours.
3. Let the children make their own magazines for clients to look through, using scrap books with favourite pictures stuck in.
4. Invite a hairdresser to visit and 'dress' hair. A parent may be willing to have a hair restyle.
5. Make a 'hairstyle' catalogue using either self-portraits or pictures cut out of magazines.
6. Read books with a focus on hair (e.g. *Topsy and Tim Have a Haircut* by Jean and Gareth Adamson, and *Rapunzel* (traditional tale).
7. Learn how to plait using soft rope.

Links to Foundation Stage Curriculum

PSE Display high levels of involvement in activities (SS)

ELG Be confident to try new activities, initiate ideas and speak in a familiar group

CLL Initiate conversation, attend to and take account of what others say, and use talk to resolve disagreements (SS)

ELG Interact with others, negotiating plans and activities and taking turns in conversation

CLL Use talk, actions and objects to recall and relive past experiences (SS)

ELG Use language to imagine and re-create roles and experiences

CLL Talk activities through, reflecting on and modifying what they are doing (SS)

ELG Use talk to organise, sequence and clarify thinking, ideas, feelings and events

PD Engage in activities requiring hand–eye coordination (SS)

ELG Handle tools, objects, construction and malleable materials safely and with increasing control

CD Pretend that one object represents another, especially when objects have characteristics in common (SS)

ELG Use imagination in art and design, music, dance, imaginative and role play and stories

CD Express and communicate ideas, thoughts and feelings by using imaginative and role play (ELG)

ACTIVITY

4 A veterinary centre

Resources you will need

- A table for examination of animals
- White and/or green tunics
- Pet boxes, baskets and cages
- Blankets for animals to lie on
- A selection of (soft toy) animals and pets (the children could supply some of these)
- Chairs for the waiting area
- A counter
- Boxes and packets of animal foods (empty and cleaned thoroughly)
- Medical equipment – stethoscope, thermometer, tweezers, syringes (no needles obviously), bandages
- Pet brushes and combs
- Pictures of domestic animals for the walls
- Leaflets about looking after a pet

Aim/concept

To help children understand the importance of caring for animals: check-ups, immunisations, grooming and so on

Process

- Look at pictures of pets and a veterinary centre with the children. Who has a pet? What do they have? Have they ever been to the vet? Why was this?
- Discuss the various reasons why pets might need to go to see the vet: check-ups, immunisations, looking poorly, not eating, limping, bad cuts.
- Discuss with the children what they might need to set up a veterinary centre in your setting.
- Help them to think about which animals would be taken to a veterinary centre (domestic pets and some injured wild animals), and which animals the vet would go to see in their own environment (e.g. farm, zoo).
- Encourage the children to bring in some animals (soft toys would be ideal). They might like to do this on a daily basis – new 'patients' each day.

Vocabulary/discussion

- Talk about the general care needs of pets, feeding, walking and exercise, grooming, replacing straw
- Use a range of animals to discuss size, differing care needs
- Name medical equipment for the children: stethoscope, tweezers, clippers, X-ray

Group size
4–6

Links to Foundation Stage Curriculum

PSE Show care and concern for others, for living things and for the environment (SS)

ELG Consider the consequences of words and actions for themselves and others

CLL Use talk to connect ideas, explain what is happening and anticipate what might happen next (SS)

ELG Use talk to imagine and re-create roles and experiences

KUW Talk about what is seen and what is happening (SS)

ELG Ask questions about why things happen and how things work

PD Show some understanding that good practices with regard to exercise, eating, sleeping and hygiene can contribute to good health (SS)

ELG Recognise the importance of keeping healthy and those things which contribute to good health

CD Pretend that one object represents another, especially when objects have characteristics in common (SS)

Extension ideas

1. Make animal paw prints by fingertip painting, using a real example as a guide.
2. Set up a mini 'Crufts' and award all the animals a prize for something.
3. Ask people to bring in pets for the children to observe and handle (e.g. dog, goat, lamb, chick, hamster, rabbit, gerbil, guinea pig, and, if possible, kittens). Always be aware of allergy issues and check with parents in advance.
4. Make a chart of who has what pets.
5. Make animal masks (see templates on pages 66–68).
6. Make a kennel from a large cardboard box.
7. Make a 'lampshade-style' collar for a dog.
8. Collect tins of pet food and give to local pet rescue centre.
9. Read books about animals, especially rescue/lost/found animals. Invite RSPCA staff to visit your children to talk about their work.
10. Access animal welfare charity information and resources for your children's age group (e.g. 'Dogs Trust' resources (www.learnwithdogs.co.uk) or 'Share the World' resources (www.sharetheworld.org.uk).

ACTIVITY 5 A pet shop

Resources you will need

- Photographs of different common domestic pets
- Posters of animals and animal foods
- Empty packets and boxes of pet foods
- Cages suitable for gerbils and rats, hutches, birdcages, fish tanks (all completely clean)
- Soft toy pets
- Rubber reptiles (e.g. snakes and geckos, plus fish)
- Till and money
- Paper bags for purchases
- Sand and scales for measuring (for budgie cages)
- A bird-table
- Leads and collars

Aim/concept

To encourage understanding of the care needs of pets and the responsibility of owning one

---

Process

- Talk about pets in general. Who has pets? What do they have? How do they help look after them?
- Show the children a range of photographs of pets. Which can they name? What can they tell you about them?
- Where do they buy pet food? How often do they buy it?
- Can they tell you what else they could buy in a pet shop?
- How would they set up a pet shop to play in themselves? Help them to identify a range of suitable resources.
- Encourage the children to bring in soft toy (pets) from home to sell or visit the pet shop.
- Encourage children to take turns in being shopkeeper and shopper.
- Model actions for cleaning out cages and tanks, and catching (plastic) fish to sell.

Vocabulary/ discussion

- Talk about pet names, types, breeds and so on
- Discuss their food, bedding and care needs
- Model how to handle the animals carefully (real or toys), showing which way to stroke them, how to pick them up, how to support them, naming each action for them

Group size

4–6

Extension ideas

1. Link to a topic on pets, or animals.
2. Set up a display of 'Our Pets', using photos or pictures.
3. Discuss hygiene and health when handling animals and their bedding, and carry out appropriate handwashing if handling animals and materials.
4. Set up a display on looking after pets, their food, grooming, bedding and exercise needs.
5. 'Clean' out a birdcage.
6. 'Clean' out a fish tank.
7. Encourage movement sessions on being pets (e.g. slithering like snakes, hopping like rabbits)
8. Read stories about owning a pet.
9. Make pet puppets using paper plates.
10. Encourage people to bring their pets into the setting, but be very aware of allergies.

Links to Foundation Stage Curriculum

PSE Display high levels of involvement in activities (SS)

ELG Be confident to try new activities, initiate ideas and speak in a familiar group

CLL Initiate conversation, attend to and take account of what others say, and use talk to resolve disagreements (SS)

ELG Interact with others, negotiating plans and activities and taking turns in conversation

CLL Use talk to connect ideas, explain what is happening and anticipate what might happen next (SS)

KUW Show an interest in the world in which they live (SS)

ELG Observe, find out about and identify features in the place they live and the natural world

PD Show some understanding that sensible practices with regard to exercise, eating, sleeping and hygiene can contribute to good health (SS)

CD Pretend that one object represents another, especially when objects have characteristics in common (SS)

ELG Use imagination in art and design, music, dance, imaginative and role play and stories

CD Express and communicate ideas, thoughts and feelings by using imaginative and role play (ELG)

ACTIVITY 6 A garden centre

Resources you will need

- Posters of plants, flowers and birds for the walls
- Low tables for display and selling
- Pot plants – indoor and outdoor varieties
- Small or artificial trees in pots
- Wooden gardening trugs (long shallow baskets for carrying flowers)
- Wicker baskets
- Gardening gloves
- Small gardening tools: forks, trowels, spades, brooms
- A child-size wheelbarrow or cart for transporting large items
- Books on gardening, plants, trees or flowers
- Ceramic plant pot holders
- Ornamental stone items

- Lightweight 'imitation' water feature bases
- If space allows: child-size garden furniture with umbrella
- Seed packets
- Bulbs (could use shallots)
- Herbs growing in pots
- Artificial flowers in buckets

Aim/concept

For children to learn about planting and harvesting according to the time of year, to choose, select and pay for items, and to increase understanding of the use of a range of utensils

Process

- Look at the photo of the garden centre on page 22.
- Who has visited one? What did they see? What did they buy?
- Discuss how garden centres sell different things at different times of year, linked to the seasons.
- Help the children to identify what they will need to set up a garden centre play setting.
- Help them to make signs and labels for their chosen items.
- Whenever possible, incorporate a planting activity within the play.
- Model actions for the children as necessary.
- Help them to choose, buy and arrange their purchases.

Vocabulary/discussion

- Talk about different seasons, and plant, flower and tree names
- Discuss the need for enriching soil, watering and natural light

Group size
4–6

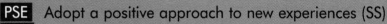

Extension ideas

1. Plant seeds and bulbs and let the children take turns to care for them.
2. Weave together long thin twigs with string to make a fence.
3. Let the children dig and handle soil (bought ready cleaned, not from the garden).
4. Measure using different sized plant pots.
5. Read books about plants and growing things (e.g. *Titch* by Pat Hutchins).
6. Make paper flowers using circles of coloured tissue paper (screwing up the middle and spreading out to create 'petals'). These could then be placed in vases or on notice-boards in the pretend garden play area.
7. Grow beans in jars.
8. Draw or paint pictures to make own flower catalogue.

Links to Foundation Stage Curriculum

PSE Adopt a positive approach to new experiences (SS)
ELG Continue to be interested, excited and motivated to learn
PSE Display high levels of involvement in activities (SS)
ELG Be confident to try new activities, initiate ideas and speak within familiar group
CLL Use talk to connect ideas, explain what is happening and anticipate what might happen next (SS)
ELG Use language to imagine and re-create roles and experiences
CLL Ascribe meanings to marks (SS)
ELG Attempt writing for different purposes, using various features such as lists, stories and instructions
MD Find items from positional/directional clues (SS)
ELG Use everyday words to describe position
KUW Examine objects and living things to find out more about them (SS)
ELG Find out about, and identify, some features of living things, objects and events which they observe
KUW Show an interest in the world in which they live (SS)
ELG Observe, find out about and identify features in the place they live and the natural world
PD Understand that equipment and tools have to be used safely (SS)
ELG Handle tools, objects, construction and malleable materials safely and with increasing control

ACTIVITY 7 A travel agent

Resources you will need

- Child-size tables and chairs
- Brochures collected from (willing) travel agents
- Posters of exotic places
- Posters showing coaches, planes and ships
- Pictures of famous places: the Eiffel Tower, Taj Mahal, Venetian gondolas, Mount Everest
- A large map of the world
- A globe
- Old passports
- Paper and pens for making bookings and taking details
- Small suitcases for travel preparations

Aim/concept

To help children find out more about the world, to increase their understanding of distance through discussions of people travelling on holiday, and to encourage making choices and decisions

Process

- Introduce the globe to the children. Who knows what it is? Can they find Britain?
- Discuss who has been to a different country. On holiday? To visit relatives? The country where they were born?
- Talk about what different places are like – hot, snowy, mountains, beaches and so on.
- How were their travels arranged? Do they know? Have they ever been to a travel agent?
- Do they know what a passport is? Or a visa?
- Show them the photographs linked to a travel agent on page 18. What can they see?
- Agree with the children what they will need to set up their own travel agent.
- Help them to set it up using the already gathered props.

Vocabulary/discussion

- Talk about places, names, environments, famous landmarks
- Talk about why these places are famous or important to a particular culture or to the world in general
- Look through holiday brochures together and discuss what the children see

Group size

4–6

Extension ideas

1. Make passports with the children using the photocopiable book template on page 71. See also page 72.
2. Make labels for suitcases.
3. Look at places around the world, using the Internet, a globe or a large map.
4. Read stories about and from around the world.
5. Learn songs from other countries.
6. Make a wall display of places the children (and staff) have visited.
7. Set up an interactive display of artefacts from around the world.
8. Set up a display on different types of travel.

Links to Foundation Stage Curriculum

PSE Display high levels of involvement in activities (SS)

ELG Be confident to try new activities, initiate ideas and speak within a familiar group

CLL Initiate conversation, attend to and take account of what others say, and use talk to resolve disagreements (SS)

CLL Use talk to connect ideas, explain what is happening and anticipate what might happen next (SS)

ELG Use language to imagine and re-create roles and experiences.

CLL Use writing as a means of recording and communicating (SS)

ELG Write things such as labels and captions

MD Find items from positional/directional clues (SS)

ELG Use everyday words to describe position

KUW Show an interest in the world in which they live (SS)

ELG Observe, find out about and identify features in the place they live and the natural world

KUW Gain an awareness of the cultures and beliefs of others (SS)

ELG Begin to know about their own cultures and beliefs and those of other people

CD Pretend that one object represents another, especially when objects have characteristics in common (SS)

ELG Use imagination in art and design, music, dance, imaginative and role play and stories

CD Express and communicate ideas, thoughts and feelings by using imaginative and role play (ELG)

ACTIVITY 8

A baby clinic

Resources you will need

- A set of weighing scales with a shallow 'bowl' on the top, suitable for laying a doll in
- Aprons for the 'nurses' and 'health visitors'
- A variety of dolls and teddy bears
- Prams and push-chairs for bringing 'babies' to the clinic
- Nappies – disposable and reusable
- Towels
- Posters of babies of different ages, baby goods and so on
- A poster about bathing a baby
- A poster about feeding a baby
- A poster about changing a nappy
- A poster about immunisations
- Toy syringes for giving 'babies' their immunisations
- Leaflets and booklets about baby care
- Growth charts for each 'baby' – see photocopiable sheet on page 73
- Tape-measures

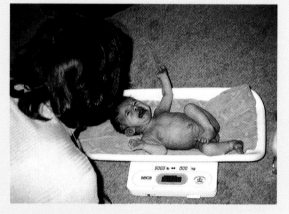

Aim/concept

For children to explore the care needs of young babies including the progress checks made on them

Process

- Look at the photograph of a baby on page 15. Who has had a baby brother or sister? Discuss their names. What else can the children tell you about them?
- Introduce the concept of a baby clinic. Can the children tell you where it might be held? Have they been there with their baby sibling? Who usually takes the baby there? What happens?
- Talk about the different checks made on the progress of a baby and also about immunisations. Can the children remember having an immunisation themselves? What can they remember about it?
- Who weighs the baby? Talk about why this is done and how it is recorded. Show the children the growth chart record sheet (page 73).
- Ask the children to think about what they would need to run a baby clinic.
- Help them to gather appropriate props and set it up.
- You may need to model some of the actions for the children initially.

Vocabulary/discussion

- Babies, names, weights, what they look like at birth, why babies are weighed
- Why immunisations are given
- Why babies are measured and how the outcomes are recorded

Group size

4–6

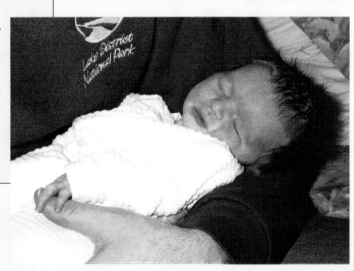

Extension ideas

1. Display 'Us as babies' photos.
2. Wash 'baby' clothes and hang them out to dry.
3. Order baby clothes by size.
4. Read books on and about babies.
5. Sing songs about babies.
6. Sort (and eat) jelly babies as a treat.
7. Leave out weighing scales as an activity to encourage estimation and comparison – provide a range of items to weigh and let children collect others. If possible, use baby-related items such as empty talc or lotion bottles, or a disposable nappy.

Links to Foundation Stage Curriculum

CLL Use talk to connect ideas, explain what is happening and anticipate what might happen next (SS)

ELG Use language to imagine and re-create roles and experiences

CLL Ascribe meanings to marks (SS)

ELG Attempt writing for different purposes, using various features such as lists, stories and instructions (SS)

MD Use some number names and number language spontaneously (SS)

Use mathematical language in play (SS)

ELG Use developing mathematical ideas and methods to solve practical problems

MD Order two items by weight or capacity (SS)

ELG Use language such as 'greater', 'smaller',' heavier' or 'lighter' to compare quantities

KUW Know how to operate simple equipment (SS)

ELG Find out about and identify the uses of everyday technology and use information to support their learning

KUW Remember and talk about significant things that have happened to them (SS)

ELG Find out about past and present events in their own lives, and in those of their families and other people they know

PD Show some understanding that good practices with regard to exercise, eating, sleeping and hygiene can contribute to good health

ELG Recognise the importance of keeping healthy and those things which contribute to good health

CD Express and communicate ideas, thoughts and feelings by using imaginative and role play (ELG)

ACTIVITY 9

A bookshop

Resources you will need

- Shelving or book stands
- Child-size tables for displaying books in piles
- Lots of books divided into categories (agreed with the children) (e.g reference, stories, poems, picture books, pop-up books, board books, cloth books, maps, books of photographs, DIY)
- A till
- Money
- Paper bags for purchases
- Catalogues of children's books – many publishers distribute these as fliers inside early years magazines; collect them throughout the year

Aims/concepts

- To foster the enjoyment of books and stories
- To encourage the concept of buying books
- To help children explore the many uses books have in life (e.g. information source, pleasure, maps, dictionaries)

Process

- Show the children the photographs on page 19. Can they tell you what sort of shop it is?
- Discuss with them how a bookshop is set out, talking about how it is divided into categories of books, how authors are usually found alphabetically.
- Who has a name beginning with 'A', 'B' and so on?
- Who has bought a book in a bookshop? What did they buy? Did they enjoy it? What can they tell you about it?
- What do the children think they need to set up their own bookshop?
- What help do they need from you?
- Help them set it up and model buying books if appropriate.

Vocabulary/discussion

- Types of books (e.g. reference, stories, poems, picture books, pop-up books, board books, cloth books, maps, books of photographs)
- Discuss what books are enjoyed by whom (e.g. babies love clear, bold images, many grown-ups like maps and photographs)
- Which are the children's favourites?

Group size

This could involve the whole group on a 'revolving' basis

Extension ideas

1. Link to a theme on books, or a special story week.
2. Increase the opportunities for reading to the children stories 'bought' by them.
3. Make books with the children – try using the photocopiable template on page 71.
4. Encourage parents and staff to bring in books with a special meaning – perhaps photographs of how the area used to look, or books in different languages.
5. Convert the bookshop into a library and include more tables (with chairs) for 'readers' to sit and 'browse', plus index cards in a box to record lending of books.
6. Convert the bookshop into a different sort of shop (e.g. a clothes shop, with stands of clothes to try on, fashion magazines to look at, hats, bags, shoes) plus a full-length mirror to admire the outcome).

Links to Foundation Stage Curriculum

PSE Display high levels of involvement in activities (SS)

ELG Be confident to try new activities, initiate ideas and speak within a familiar group

CLL Use talk to connect ideas, explain what is happening and anticipate what might happen next (SS)

ELG Use language to imagine and re-create roles and experiences

CLL Show interest in illustrations and print in books, and print in the environment (SS)

ELG Be aware that print carries meaning and, in English, is read from left to right and top to bottom

CLL Begin to be aware of the way stories are structured (SS)

Be aware that information can be relayed in the form of print (SS)

Enjoy an increasing range of books (SS)

ELG Show an understanding of the elements of stories, such as main character, sequence of events and openings, and how information may be found in non-fiction texts to answer questions about where, who, why and how

MD Find items from positional/directional clues (SS)

ELG Use everyday words to describe position

PD Engage in activities requiring hand–eye coordination (SS)

ELG Handle tools, objects, construction and malleable materials safely and with increasing control

ACTIVITY 10   A supermarket

Resources you will need

- Boxes and packages collected in advance and stuffed with newspaper to help keep their shape
- Pretend foods, such as fruits, vegetables, eggs, bread, pizza, either made from salt dough (see page 62) or purchased commercially
- Washed-out containers of (safe) products (e.g. washing liquids, washing-up liquids, sauces, salad creams, fruit juice cartons, milk containers
- Tills, money and shopping baskets
- Posters of food products

Aims/concepts

- For children to take on familiar roles from their own experience
- To handle money, giving and receiving payment and change
- To write for a purpose

Process

- Talk to the children about supermarkets. Who shops at one? When do they go there? How often? What do they buy?
- Ask them to explain what is different about a supermarket compared with a smaller shop. Help them to compare and contrast their ideas.
- Talk about shopping in general. What do they like about shopping? What do they dislike?
- How could they make a supermarket themselves? What do they need?
- Help them to set up a suitable role-play area.
- Model buying and selling for them, giving and receiving change.

Vocabulary/discussion

- Discuss different products, helping the children categorise them into foods, cleaning products, baby goods and so on
- Talk about the difference in size of supermarkets compared with other shops.
- Talk about layout, accessibility of goods, room for trolleys
- Discuss money values

Group size
4–6

Extension ideas

1. Link to theme on food.
2. Set up a range of activities on healthy eating.
3. Make a food 'wheel' showing the main food groups.
4. Make a chart with the children of who eats what for breakfast.
5. Sort a range of food packets by one feature (e.g. needs cooking/is frozen).
6. Provide scales and a range of food items for weighing, and ask the children to place them in order of heaviness.

Links to Foundation Stage Curriculum

PSE Display high levels of involvement in activities (SS)
ELG Be confident to try new activities, initiate ideas and speak within a familiar group
CLL Consistently develop a simple story, explanation or line of questioning (SS)
ELG Speak clearly and audibly with confidence and control and show awareness of the listener (e.g. by their use of conventions such as greetings, 'please' and 'thank you')
MD Use mathematical language in play (SS)
ELG Say and use number names in order in familiar contexts
KUW Know how to operate simple equipment (SS)
ELG Find out about and identify the uses of everyday technology, and use information and communication technology to support their learning
KUW Show an interest in the world in which they live (SS)
ELG Observe, find out about and identify features in the place they live and in the natural world
KUW Notice differences between the features of the local environment (SS)
ELG Find out about their environment, and talk about those features they like and dislike
CD Pretend that one object represents another, especially when objects have characteristics in common (SS)
ELG Use imagination in art and design, music, dance, imaginative and role play and stories
CD Express and communicate ideas, thoughts and feelings by using imaginative and role play (ELG)

ACTIVITY 11 A post office

Resources you will need

- A post box (see page 59 for ideas)
- A counter for serving
- Scales and weights
- Letters and parcels of different sizes and weights
- A till and money
- Stamps (sheets of stickers may be used instead)
- Old receipt pads or note pads
- Old benefit books (all personal details removed)
- Pens
- Rubber stamps and ink pads
- Goods for sale (e.g. envelopes, paper, pens, cards)
- A bag suitable for the postman or postwoman to use

Aims/concepts

- For children to learn the process of sending letters and parcels
- To learn about weighing items and to handle money
- To 'write' for a purpose (e.g. writing a letter and 'posting' it)

Process

- Introduce the photographs on page 14. Who knows what they are?
- What can the children tell you about the post office? What do they buy there? What else can people do there?
- Who can tell you who works for the post office?
- Who has seen postal workers on their rounds? What can they tell you about them?
- Who likes receiving letters? When do they receive the most (e.g. festival days, birthdays)?
- What would they need to set up their own post office?
- Where could they gather resources from?
- Help them to set up a suitable area.

Vocabulary/discussion

- Talk about the role of the post office, and how important it is to keeping people in touch
- Discuss the various services provided by the post office
- Ask the children what they buy at the post office, and who likes to send and receive post

Group size

4–6

Extension ideas

1. Help each child to send a letter to another child within the setting, ensuring that all children receive a letter.

2. Use a pile of old stamps and classify by type.

3. Look at a collection of stamps and talk about where in the world they came from.

4. Use a globe or map to find the countries for each stamp.

5. Encourage other people to send post to the children in the setting.

6. Make a post-box from a large container and encourage its use for posting, taking turns to sort and deliver 'post'.

7. Make up parcels and weigh them – folded-up newspapers, blocks of packaging, books and boxes are useful items to wrap.

8. Write letters home to families and friends.

9. Make envelopes from coloured paper – an excellent folding activity which encourages dexterity.

Links to Foundation Stage Curriculum

PSE Display high levels of involvement in activities (SS)

ELG Be confident to try new activities, initiate ideas and speak within a familiar group

CLL Use talk to connect ideas, explain what is happening and anticipate what might happen next (SS)

ELG Use language to imagine and re-create roles and experiences

CLL Talk activities through, reflecting on and modifying what they are doing (SS)

ELG Use talk to organise, sequence and clarify thinking, ideas, feelings and events

CLL Ascribe meanings to marks (SS)
Use writing as a means of recording and communicating (SS)

ELG Attempt writing for different purposes, using various features such as lists, stories and instructions

ELG Write their own names and other things, such as labels and captions

MD Order two items by weight or capacity (SS)

ELG Use language such as 'greater', 'smaller', 'heavier' or 'lighter' to compare quantities (SS)

CD Express and communicate ideas, thoughts and feelings by using imaginative and role play (ELG)

ACTIVITY

12 Air travel

Resources you will need

- Globe or large map of the world
- Photographs of different types of planes
- Chairs set out in rows
- Round 'window' drawings to attach to the walls
- 'Smart' uniforms (with hats) for the flight attendants
- Steering wheel, gear stick and 'controls' panel for the pilot
- Trolleys
- Bags and small suitcases
- Lap trays and resources for serving meals
- Headphones
- 'Tickets', passports and luggage labels
- Area for weighing in the luggage

Aim/concept

To enable children to build on their own travel experiences and explore new ideas about travel

Process

- Look at pictures and photographs of planes and airports.
- What can the children tell you? Who has been on a plane? Who has been to an airport? Where did they go? What did they do? Travel? Meet or see somebody off?
- Use the globe or map to point out how far they have travelled. Always ensure you show them where they live now.
- Help them to think of the different jobs people have (e.g. pilot, flight attendant, baggage handler, ticket sales/checking, passport control).
- Who has a passport? What does it look like? Why do they need one? What does it allow them to do? What happens to their passport? Show them a real one.
- Talk to the children about sitting on a plane for long periods of time, the meals, seat-belts, keeping safe during take-off and landing. Help them to think about the angle they will be sitting at during these times.
- Do they know what will happen when they arrive at their destination? Discuss this with them.
- Encourage the children to tell you how they could set out the cabin of a plane in their role-play area. What would they need?
- Help them to collect the resources they will need.
- Make passports for each child (you may like to use the photocopiable sheet on page 72).
- Model play with them as appropriate, encouraging the children to change roles to broaden their experience.
- Set up a departure lounge with comfortable seats.

Vocabulary/discussion

- Discuss the different roles of people involved in flight
- Talk about passports, visas and so on
- Discuss destinations. Where have the children been? Where have you been? Where would they choose to go? Why? What appeals to them about a specific place? Could they get there any other way? How?
- Talk about airports (e.g. the size, bustling atmosphere, public address systems, what happens in arrivals)

Group size

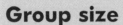

8–10

Extension ideas

1. Link to a topic on travel.
2. Read stories about flying (e.g. *Going on a Plane* by Anne Civardi and Stephen Cartwright).
3. Make a display of the world, adding place names that the children know or have visited.
4. Make a display of holiday photographs.
5. Enjoy movement sessions linked to being planes, helicopters and other forms of transport.
6. Practise carrying trays of plastic cups like a flight attendant. Who can keep them balanced?
7. Eat lunch or snacks on 'airline' lap trays.

Links to Foundation Stage Curriculum

PSE Display high levels of involvement in activities (SS)

ELG Be confident to try new activities, initiate ideas and speak within a familiar group

CLL Initiate conversation, attend to and take account of what others say, and use talk to resolve disagreements (SS)

ELG Interact with others, negotiating plans and activities and taking turns in conversation

CLL Use talk to connect ideas, explain what is happening and anticipate what might happen next (SS)

ELG Use language to imagine and re-create roles and experiences

KUW Show an interest in the world in which they live (SS)

ELG Observe, find out about and identify features in the place they live and in the natural world

CD Pretend that one object represents another, especially when objects have characteristics in common (SS)

ELG Use imagination in art and design, music, dance, imaginative and role play and stories

CD Express and communicate ideas, thoughts and feelings by using imaginative and role play (ELG)

Making props

This section offers simple-to-follow instructions for making a range of useful props to support role play:

- Rooms and 'buildings'
- Clothes
- Food
- Jewellery

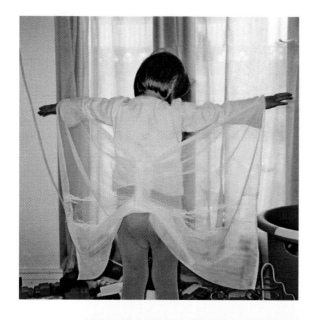
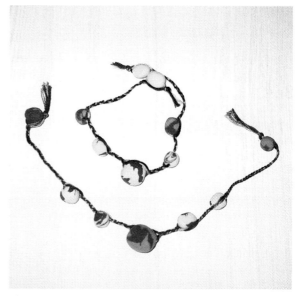

As you gather together a range of props, it is important to remember that:

- All props need to be able to be cleaned easily and frequently.
- Hats can harbour head infestations and so need particular attention.
- A variety of different fastenings will encourage skill development, useful in dressing and undressing.
- Easy fastenings are ideal for the youngest children to support and promote independence.
- Generous-sized outfits avoid disappointments and again help support independence.
- Clothes should reflect and provide for both culture and gender.
- Accessories such as bags, shoes and jewellery are great favourites.
- Masks and helmets are often popular, so whenever practical have plenty.

Be aware that:

- Not all children are happy to wear masks.
- Some children may be alarmed by others wearing a mask.

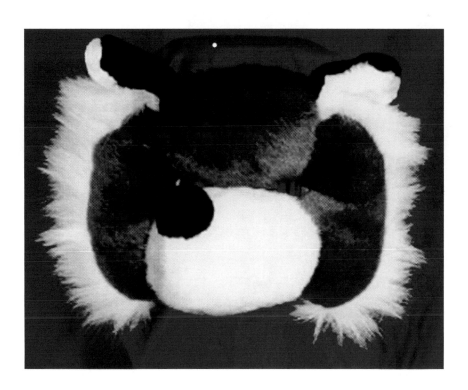

Commercial props

There are many wonderful props available commercially that can enhance and encourage role play. The following examples have been supplied by East–West Education and Stompers. Details of these and other companies may be found on page 76.

Promote and value a range of cultures by providing outfits from different parts of the world.

Adult outfits are also available.

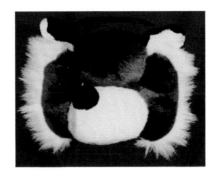

Let your children's imaginations run wild, or enjoy themed play as a group.

Ideas for props

Use lengths of material.

Try to provide lengths of interesting material for the children to encourage them to imagine and to wrap themselves up however they wish.

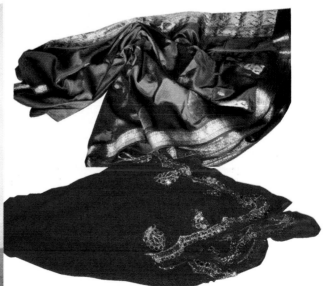

A pop-over-the-head sari

(NB: All pieces of the following garment will need hemming before construction.)

- Cut a length of material 130cm wide x 50cm (waist to ankles).
- Machine stitch three soft folds in the middle (front), sewing along the top edge, and join edges to form the back seam.

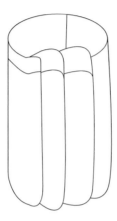

- Cut a length of material 60cm x 30cm to make the bodice. Place 'off centre' along the front and back edges with a 2cm gap on the right-hand side of the garment.
- Cut a long length of material 115cm x 30cm. Machine this into a tube shape and turn right-side out.
- Attach this to the front edge at the same time as the bodice piece (this length will flow over the child's left shoulder).

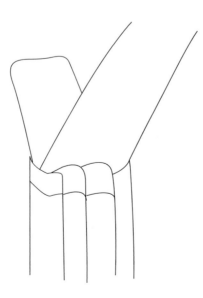

- Machine stitch a 'gather' along the top shoulder edge of the bodice piece.
- The 'sari' is now ready to pop over the head.

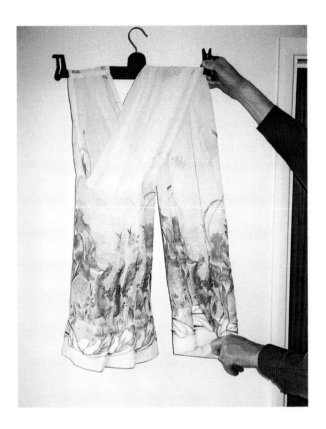 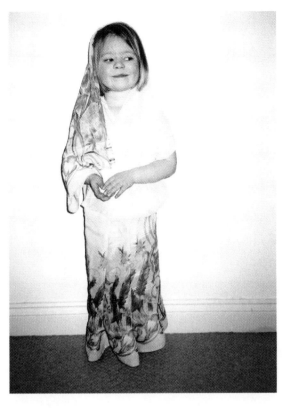

Basic tabard

This versatile tabard shape may be used to make coveralls for cooking, or as a base for themed outfits that are simple to put on. Ideal examples would include a nurse's or Red Indian outfit.

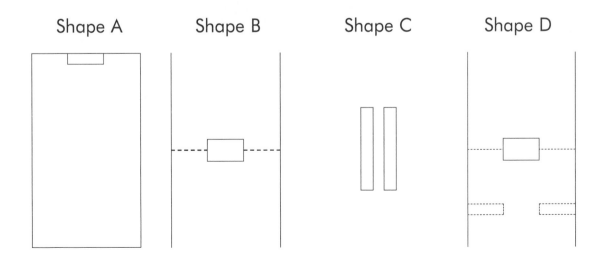

Shape A   Shape B   Shape C   Shape D

- As a pattern guide, use the wrapper from a ream of copier paper opened out flat (55cm x 39cm).
- Cut four of shape A and join at the shoulders to make two of shape B, and two 'bands' to attach to the sides (C).
- Position bands to sides of tabard (on the right side).
- Machine both sides of tabard shape, leaving bottom edges raw.
- Turn pieces right way out and iron flat (shape D).
- Turn neck edges inwards and machine stitch close to the edge for a neat finish. Make a tiny snip in each corner before sewing, to 'ease' the fabric.
- Turn 'hem' edges inwards and again sew close to the edges.
- Attach Velcro to ends of tabs and corresponding side of tabard.
- Iron flat.

(NB: A basic cape can easily be made from an adult skirt by opening up a seam and hemming the raw edges, attaching a fastening at the neck.)

Butterfly wings

These simple wings may be used for butterfly or fairy play. Ideally they can be made from pieces of net curtain.

- Cut a length of net curtain 90cm x 65cm.
- Machine stitch all edges neatly.
- Make a loop of net material 40cm long x 15cm wide.
  - This (loosely) gathers the middle of the 'wings', being sewn securely at the top edge (the final step in the process).

Either:

- Use net curtains with a lace design (as shown), *or*
- Design a symmetrical pattern on each wing using a colourful material. If possible, attach the design to both sides, so that the wings may be used either way round.

Finally:

- Machine stitch a loop of elastic to the top edge of both wing tips. These will be held by the child's thumb or around their wrist as they 'fly'.

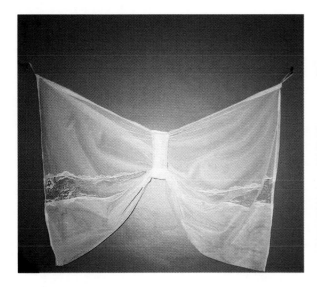 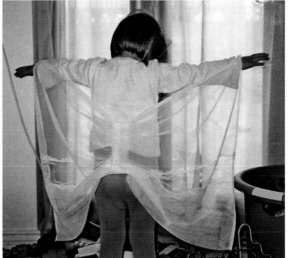

Play pyjamas

This basic-shape outfit may be used as a basis for many outfits, depending on the type and colour of material used and any accessories added to it.

Using the pattern on photocopiable page 74, cut out all the pieces.

For the top:

- Join back to front at shoulders.
- Join top of sleeves to 'armholes'.
- Cut a 20cm slit from top of front neck downwards.
- Make a fold in front (5cm over 5cm) to make an overlap for the Velcro fastening.
- Machine stitch the overlap into place by sewing under the opening (5cm across).
- Machine sides and sleeves.
- Cut bias neck edges by measuring the length of the neck opening and cutting a 5cm-wide length diagonally across spare material. This enables the material to be 'eased' slightly as you sew.
- Hem sleeve and bottom edges.
- Sew Velcro to opening.

For the trousers:

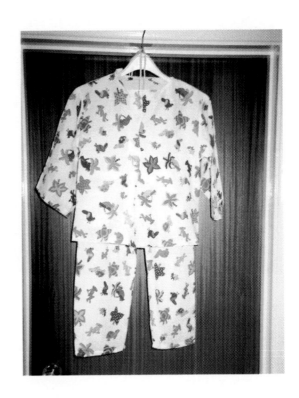

- Machine stitch central body seam on each 'leg'.
- Join at inside legs.
- Machine stitch outside of each leg.
- Hem bottoms of each leg.
- Turn over waistband edge and machine stitch.
- Thread elastic through the waistband and secure firmly.

Ideas using large cardboard boxes

Large cardboard boxes are always a great favourite with young children. Their imagination can turn the boxes into cars, rockets or dens, and items of machinery such as a television or a washing machine.

Boxes are often discarded as containers of 'white' goods such as washing machines or dishwashers, or of television and computer equipment. Ask around to see who has them to spare.

Try helping the children to turn boxes into items of their choice, or use them in themed play activities (e.g telephone or post box, petrol pump, car).

Role-play areas

When you are helping the children to make a role-play area, think about the use of partitions:

- Drapes such as old curtains that can be fixed into place securely to give privacy are ideal.
- A table or an A-frame climbing frame may be useful. These can provide simple but effective structures.
- Use old curtains or lengths of material to create enclosed spaces which give the children a sense of secrecy.
- Try adding silver stars to the underside of a dark 'roof' to make a night-time sky.
- Decorate a 'roof' with fruits and flowers to enjoy an aspect of the Jewish Feast of Tabernacles and the building of a sukkot.
- Try adding straw to the 'roof' to make a stable for a farm or nativity play.

Windows with views

A simple way of changing the emphasis of a role-play area can be to add a window with a view.

- Paint a view, or purchase a large poster of an interesting place.
- Cut out a large window-frame shape to fit the picture.
- Attach securely and Blu-tack to the wall.

Try:

- A seaside scene for a café.
- A countryside scene for *Three Bears Cottage* play.
- A street of shops for town house play.
- Clouds and sky for plane or hot-air balloon play.

Try varying the scene slightly once the children have gone home or out to lunch, changing from sunny weather to rain or snow. Watch how their play and discussion change.

Jewellery

Most children love to dress up in jewellery. It can be great fun to allow them to make their own and to develop lots of dexterity skills along the way. There are many different materials that may be used to make jewellery. Try using:

- Air-dry clay
- Fimo
- Kaylite
- Papier mâché
- Foil bottle tops

Clay, Fimo and Kaylite need to be moulded into appropriate shapes and a small hole pierced through the shapes. Clay and Fimo dry completely hard, but can sometimes chip with constant use.

Kaylite has the benefit of remaining slightly flexible. Details of this material may be found on page 76.

Papier mâché and air-dry clay need time to dry, so these activities will need to be planned in advance.

Bottle tops can be collected by the children and brought into the setting. They can often be the simplest material for younger children to use.

- When a range of 'beads' has been made, enjoy threading the beads on to string or shoe-laces.
- Older children will enjoy learning to plait, and can plait their strings in between beads. This can give a more professional finish.

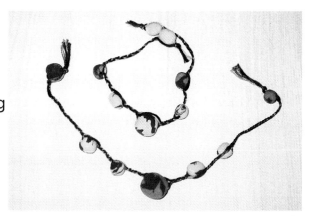

Jewellery boxes can be made by sticking small shells firmly on to wooden boxes. A strong glue is needed for this. Try varnishing them afterwards. Again this will need to be planned in advance.

Salt dough

Salt dough may be used to make food and other items useful in role play. Try making a range of foods using the recipe below. Ideal foods to make include bread rolls, biscuits, naan breads, eggs, sausages, samosas, vegetables (e.g. carrots, potatoes, courgettes) and fruits (e.g. apples, pears, plums and strawberries).

Salt dough recipe

Ingredients:

- 1 cup of salt
- Approximately $^1/_4$ of a cup of water
- 1 cup of cornflour
- $^1/_2$ cup of water

Method:

- Mix together salt and $^1/_4$ of a cup of water in a saucepan.
- Stir constantly over a medium heat for 3–4 minutes until the mixture bubbles.
- Remove from the heat and immediately stir in the cornflour and $^1/_2$ a cup of water.
- Stir until stiff.
- Knead well until pliable.
- Store in an airtight container until needed.

The mixture will harden if exposed to the air in 36 hours, or may be baked in an oven at 180c and painted.

Photocopiable sheets

Tying a sari

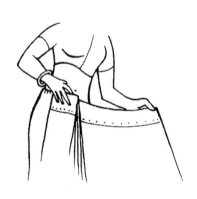

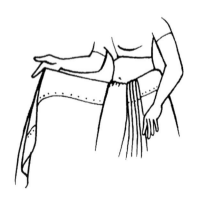

© Sandy Green (2005) *Role Play*, published by David Fulton Publishers Ltd.

Tying a turban

© Sandy Green (2005) *Role Play*, published by David Fulton Publishers Ltd.

A mask template

© Sandy Green (2005) *Role Play*, published by David Fulton Publishers Ltd.

A mask template

© Sandy Green (2005) *Role Play*, published by David Fulton Publishers Ltd.

A mask template

© Sandy Green (2005) *Role Play*, published by David Fulton Publishers Ltd.

Sheet of menu orders

Order for table _____

Order for table _____

Order for table _____

Order for table _____

© Sandy Green (2005) *Role Play*, published by David Fulton Publishers Ltd.

A sample menu

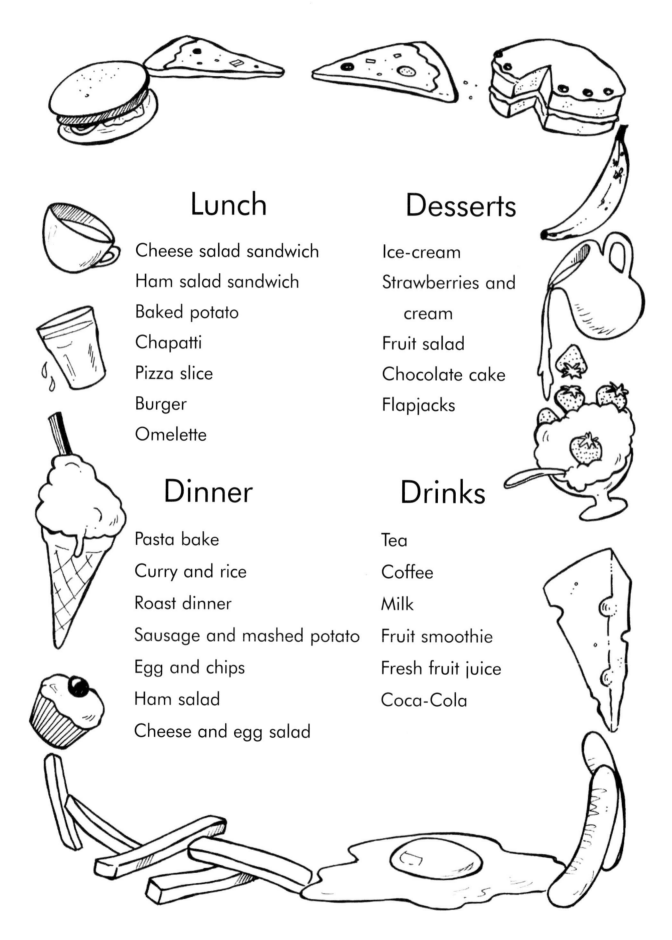

Lunch

Cheese salad sandwich

Ham salad sandwich

Baked potato

Chapatti

Pizza slice

Burger

Omelette

Desserts

Ice-cream

Strawberries and
cream

Fruit salad

Chocolate cake

Flapjacks

Dinner

Pasta bake

Curry and rice

Roast dinner

Sausage and mashed potato

Egg and chips

Ham salad

Cheese and egg salad

Drinks

Tea

Coffee

Milk

Fruit smoothie

Fresh fruit juice

Coca-Cola

© Sandy Green (2005) *Role Play*, published by David Fulton Publishers Ltd.

Making a book

1. An A4 sheet held landscape.

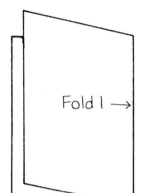

2. Fold the A4 sheet in half, with the fold on the right.

Fold 1 →

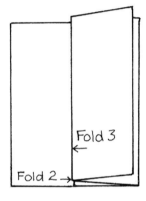

Fold 3 ←

Fold 2 →

3. Fold the two sides outwards towards the central fold. Open the furthest side out again. You should now have one layer of paper on the left and three on the right.

4. Fold in half towards you.

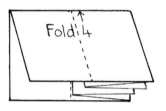

Fold 4

5. Open up again (as in stage 2 with fold again on your right).
Cut half-way along the horizontal fold, from the right to the left.

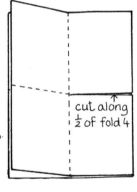

cut along ½ of fold 4

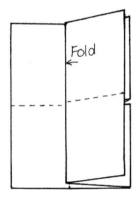

Fold ←

6. Fold as in stage 3. You should have one layer of paper on the left and three layers on the right.

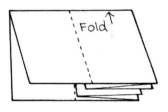

Fold

7. Fold in half downwards, towards you once again.

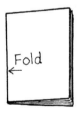

Fold ←

8. Fold in half again sideways to form a book shape.

© Sandy Green (2005) *Role Play*, published by David Fulton Publishers Ltd.

A passport

EUROPEAN UNION

**UNITED KINGDOM OF
GREAT BRITAIN
AND NORTHERN IRELAND**

PASSPORT

© Sandy Green (2005) *Role Play*, published by David Fulton Publishers Ltd.

A baby's growth chart

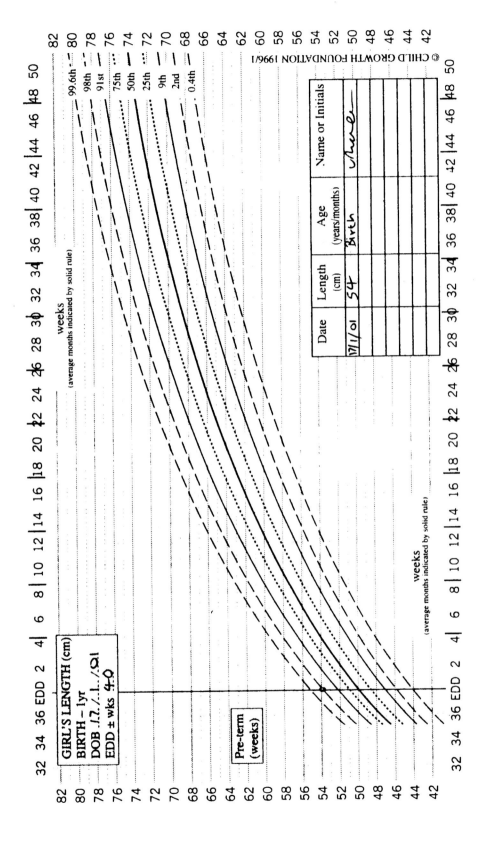

Play pyjamas

A useful way of measuring pattern pieces accurately is to set them out onto graph paper.

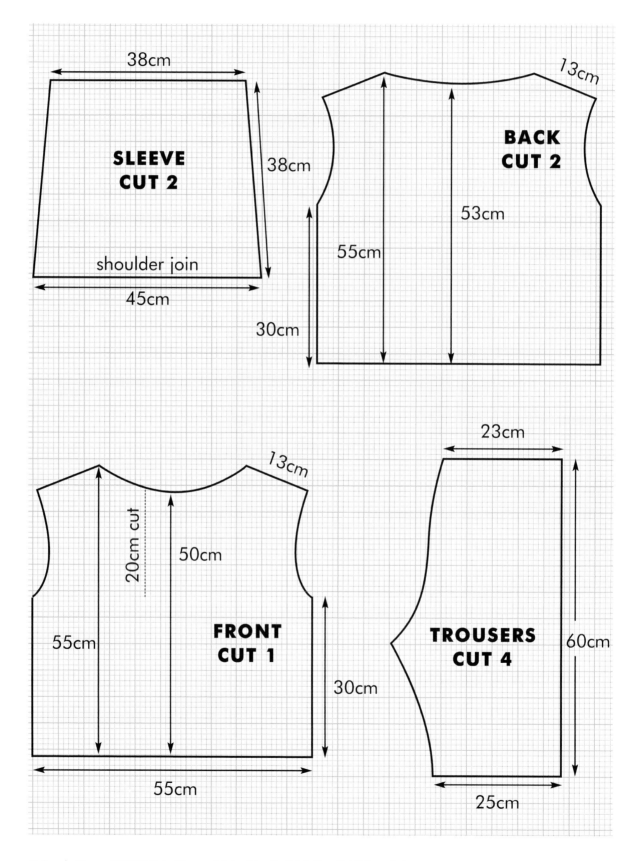

© Sandy Green (2005) *Role Play*, published by David Fulton Publishers Ltd.

References and suggested reading

Jean Adamson and Gareth Adamson, *Topsy and Tim* books (Ladybird)

Jo Boulton and Judith Ackroyd, *Pirates and Other Adventures* (David Fulton)

Jo Boulton and Judith Ackroyd, *The Toymaker's Workshop and Other Tales* (David Fulton)

Jo Boulton and Judith Ackroyd, *The Teddy Bears' Picnic and Other Stories* (David Fulton)

Tina Bruce, *Time to Play in Early Childhood Education* (Hodder & Stoughton)

Pat Hutchins, *Titch* (The Bodley Head)

Judith Kerr, *The Tiger Who Came to Tea* (HarperCollins Picture Lions)

Michael Rosen, *We're Going on a Bear Hunt* (Walker)

Anne Civardi and Stephen Cartwright, *Going on a Plane* (Usbourne)

Traditional, *Goldilocks and the Three Bears*

Traditional, *Rapunzel*

Traditional, *The Three Billy Goats Gruff*

Traditional, *The Three Little Pigs*

Resources and stockists

East–West Education (EWE)
3 Keymer Gardens
Burgess Hill
West Sussex
RH15 0AF
www.eastwesteducation.org

GALT Educational and Pre-school
Johnsonbrook Road
Hyde
Cheshire
SK1 4QT
enquiries@galt-educational.co.uk

Kaylite modelling material (non-toxic)
Newclay Products Ltd
1 Battle Road
Newton Abbot
Devon
TQ12 6RY
www.newclay.co.uk

Stompers
32 Poplar Grove
New Malden
Surrey
KT3 3DE
www.stompers.co.uk

Three Bears Playthings
Steward House
High Street
Rothbury
Northumberland
NE65 7TL
www.threebearsplaythings.co.uk